Ozark Mountain Tales

By Peggy Lee Johnson

© 2013 print edition

Any similarities to people living or dead are purely a coincidence. But they may be my neighbors .

Ozark Mountain Tales
Chapter 1
Cletus's Christmas

Cletus measured and marked off the wall inside the trailer making sure there was plenty of room near the ceiling. Picking up the chainsaw, he pulled on the rope starter until finally it roared to life, blue plumes of smoke quickly filled the living room. "Cletus, just how long you gonna have that there thing running in here. Gassing me and the kids out!"

Smiling he kept on cutting until finally daylight began to peek from the cuts. Standing up he shut the roaring machine off and laid it on the living room floor. With one swift kick, the wall lay out in the driveway. The room was silent.

"So just how you gonna keep the dogs out till morning anyway?"

Cletus grinned and opened the bag, inside was a folded blue tarp. "I dun thought of that too. See we just going to hang this here up and nail it to the floor until morning. Gonna be bright sunny day a morrow, finish it then. Hey you boys best be leaving it alone too or how's Ole Saint Nick gonna get in?"

All six kids stood there nodding. Brenda Sue handed him nails and stood back admiring the work. "You're doing a fine job Honey. Now let's go on at bed. We all can get her done tomorrow."

Wasn't long and everyone was asleep. The winds outside began to blow and white light flakes of snow began to cover the ground. Gusts caught the tarp and it blew into the house, snow accumulating on the floor. All night it snowed and blowed until by morning the living room was covered.

Cletus felt the chill and slipped out from under the massive pile of quilts. "Dang furnace must be off again. Durn fine way for a man to have at get woke up."

He closed the door behind him so Brenda Sue didn't wake up with war paint first thing. Stumbling to the kitchen, he filled the coffee pot with water, threw in a good amount of coffee and turned on the gas stove. A sharp blast of cold air turned him around. Walking into the living room, he couldn't believe his eyes, snow was waist deep, covering his TV and most of the sofa. The pine tree so carefully cut from behind the shed was covered in fluffy white snow, the Christmas lights blinking eerily beneath it. Joe Bob still in his long johns had a dishpan, filling it with the fresh white snow.

"What in tarnation are you doing Joe Bob? Get back in your room and put some clothes on boy! Go get Billy Bob and your brothers. Let's get this here outta the room for your mama gets up."

The boy scurried off towards the back bedroom.

"Hey guys! Ya'll had better get up. Dad done messed up the TV room and we got us snow!"

Hurriedly five boys uncovered their heads and stared at their little brother. "We know it snowed you dog. Now go on and get for I get up and pound on you!"

Billy Bob, ya'll better come on, I'm not kidding you, the living room's full of snow! The Christmas tree almost buried in it. Come see what Dad did! Momma gonna kill him for sure!"

So now we have six boys, all-jumping around, throwing on long handles and jeans running to see the snow. They stood at the doorway, jaws dropped; "Man Dad, Moms gonna be mad at you this time for sure. I never saw so much snow. Wow!"

Cletus frowned raising an eyebrow at the group. "Get the broom and some pans; let's get this here outta here! She gonna be mad and not just at me, so If I was ya'll I'd get going!" Within minute's brooms mops, dishpans, skillets all tools of the moment banged around the room. The floor was frozen slick as slime on a frog pond. Billy Bob disappeared into the back bedroom again followed by his brothers. Cletus started towards the front of the trailer to open the door and sweep out the remaining snow. A slick plastic shopping bag hidden beneath the snowy gift gave him a slip and a slide and slammed him into the wall. The picture of Grandpa John Henry smashed to the floor. Then he heard it a dreaded horrid sound.

"If I gotta come outta this room ya'll gonna be wishing you was back in school. I don't know what you boys are doing but knock it off! Cletus! What in tarnation going on in there?"

Cletus stood up and slid sideways again landing on the coffee table, the lamp crashed to the floor.

Then the sound of slamming doors and footsteps. The forty-five foot trailer house echoed. Silence followed. He heard the back bedroom door creak. "Them boys gonna leave it to me they are. I going to do me some whopping, I going to do me some butt burning. "

He mumbled knowing what was coming next. Silence.

"Oh my Heavens, Oh my Cletus, just what are you doing? My lamp! That was my Aunt Vera's lamp, it over 6 years old, it's a collector's piece. How could you do this? Look at my floor! Where are the boys? What have you done to my house?"

Laying there sprawled on the wet slippery floor he smiled up at her. "Why what you think I doing blast you. You think I like lying around in my underwear in the snow. Blast it woman! Help me up. My long handles are plum soaked."

Brenda Sue reached her hand down to him shaking her head. "You best have a good explanation for this!"

Cletus looked at the flapping tarp behind him, "What you think happed Brenda Sue? Take a look at that tarp! We got us a regular blizzard out there and no wall! Why I have me a mind to go down to that there radio station and give Henry that there weather guesser, a piece of my mind. Warm and dry!"

Suddenly there was a banging noise from down the hall. Brenda Sue let go of Cletus hand and headed towards the sounds. Cletus on his hands and knees crawled towards the dry kitchen floor and boiling coffee sizzling on the stove. Brown boiling grounds now dripping down the front of the stove, the flame trying to say lit.

The trailer hose was now completely silent as he watched her turn the doorknob and open the boy's bedroom door. He saw her put her hands on her hips and prepared himself for what was next. He knew it was coming, recognized the look and stance of a madwoman.

Six boys' three sets of bunk beds and snow piled on every piece of furniture they could use. Bowls, pans and skillets now held the precious melting white slush. "Oh my, I just don't know what. I am gonna have the hide off ever one of you. Get your rear ends in gear and get that outta here. This minute. Ya'll better stop sitting there with your faces hanging out and move it. Now!"

As if a bolt a lightning from the Good Lord himself had struck the lots of them they moved. All six boys running with pans of what was once snow. Water splashed on the hall carpet. The bathtub was full of the stuff too. Brenda Sue threw open the back door and pointed. "Throw it out the door you heathens! Stop spilling it all over my... Oh my heavens. Cletus! Do something!"

Standing firmly on dry ground taking a deep breath he moved towards the scene of the crime. "Okay boys. Everybody stop right where you are and I do mean now!"

Again that bolt of lighten look and everyone stopped. Terror filled their faces. Cletus, trying as hard as he could to frown, but a curl formed at the corner of his mouth. "Okay boys. Now, no body gonna die today. Not on my shift they ain't. Now lets slowly, one at a time dump out the slush. Billy Bob, you go on out to the kitchen and empty the sink. You boys walk. There you go. Dump it out. There we are now. See ain't that easier?"

Cletus walked back to the kitchen, the boys filing past him to their room once again. Brenda Sue plopped down on a chair and frowned; "This is all your fault you know. You and them there bright ideas! You best be getting that wood burner done today. Ain't no use trying to warm this here place at all till you gets a wall back in."

Leaning back in the wooden chair he rolled a smoke and let the bluish streams circle his head. His breath billowing steam in the kitchen air. "You just go on in the room. Get dressed make some vittles and I'll have her done in no time. Quit worrying that pretty little head a yours."

Cletus opened the large box and slipped the fireplace parts out on the frozen floor. Soon he was surrounded by six boy childs, all wanting to help make amends for their behavior. Cletus barked orders and within two hours, the wall was back in place. The fireplaces insert, glowing all brassy against the paneled walls. Jim Bob the middle boy carried in an armload of wood and dumped it in front of Cletus. "I got them from the shed Dad. Might get them to burn right nicely."

Cletus took his small axe and broke one into smaller pieces, a small indention showing on the linoleum floor.

"Ought to do just fine boy. Good job."

Brenda Sue pulled the kitchen chair into the doorway between the two rooms and watched as Cletus and his almost grown up pile of boy childs worked. They got the caulking gun out and sealed up the cracks around the fireplace and the aluminum trailer walls. Then he nailed up the broken pieces of paneling to almost perfect fit. One by one all the boys circled their Dad who was steadily finishing the magic. He knelt down and laid the lit match to the pile of newspapers under the split woods. A tiny red glow began to grown and before long, the wood crackled and smoked. They boys cheered and applauded Cletus.

Brenda Sue got up and walked over to the circle of testosterone in all its manly glory. The hunters celebrating their first fire. Smiling down and touching him gently on the shoulder she whispered; "Cletus this is gonna be the best Christmas ever."

Chapter 2
UNCLE BEN'S SALSA

Brenda Sue threw open the front door and blue gray smoke billowed out into the cold night air. "Cletus! You said you'd get that blasted chimney fixed! It's plum dark out and now you tell me you and the boys going deer hunting. If it ain't fixed by tomorrow afternoon there is gonna be hell to pay around here!"

Cletus pulled his heavy snow boots on and zipped up his coveralls. "No worries Brenda Sue. I'll be picking' up that box of chimney parts at the hardware tomorrow first thing. They told me all I needed was a thing called a damper. I never knew furnaces could be so complicated, did you? Anyway, the boys and me been planning this all week. I ain't about to back down this late in the game. Sides that, you was wanting some venison for Christmas dinner. We'll get ya a big fat one, enough at feed that hoard of a family you got coming' over."

Brenda Sue slowly closed the door just as a set of headlights turned down the long gravel drive way. "I think your so called buddies are here for you. Just go on and get cause I ain't having all them tracking' up my new linoleum floor."

After dropping off her man and his buddies, Becky Lee waved at Brenda and turned the big Chevy wagon around then headed back up the driveway. Cletus grabbed his sack and the shotgun from the wall. "Come here woman, and kiss me good bye. There'll be fresh meat in this house tonight!"

Brenda Sue smiled and gave him a quick peck on the cheek and slapped him on his backside. "Go get out of here, Cletus. Get your mighty hunter self outta here."

Standing there in the driveway was LeRoy, Oatis, Billy Bob and little Black Billy wearing camos and each carrying their gear and shotguns. Cletus pulled the door shut and headed towards the tarp-covered truck parked out beside the trailer.

"Come on LeRoy and help me get my old' Charger uncovered. She's all gassed up and ready to go."

LeRoy and Oatis grabbed edges and slowly the tarp revealed Cletus's pride and joy, painted all camouflaged with shiny chrome roll guards. It had lights along the top and plenty of seating room in the back. Billy Bob helped fold the tarp and noticed the roof was missing. "Hey Cletus, where's the top for this, anyway? Would be a mite warmer riding' if ya put it back on, ya know."

Cletus pointed at the large ditch back of the shed; "Kids used it as a sled and forgot to bring it back. Buried under all that snow we got the other night. Besides that, if we put it on you guys couldn't stand up and spot light any good deer, now could ya?"

LeRoy, Oatis, and Black Billy climbed in the back of the truck. Billy Bob and Cletus were in front. "Okay boys, I figure we can head on over to Uncle Ben's place. It's been up for sale now for a year. Should have us a mighty good herd of bambies by now. Gonna cut across the field if ya feel up to it."

LeRoy reached down and patted Cletus's orange baseball cap. "Get her done, mighty leader. Night time's a wasting' sitting here. Sides that we don't get outta here soon Brenda Sue's gonna come out and start asking' questions. You bring some beers, didn't ya?"

Cletus pointed over his shoulder. "Yep, in the cooler your standing' on. Ya'll ready?"

Wasn't long and the big V-8 rumbled off down the driveway, its four-wheel drive cutting deep ruts into the half thawed farm field. The night sky was clear and black. The stars were shining silently down on the bloodthirsty group of hunters as they splashed off into the woods.

"Hey Cletus! Look yonder, there towards Ben's place; I see lights there. I thought ya said Uncle Ben was gone and this place was empty. Looking to me like maybe ya got some squatters yonder. Let's go check it out!"

Shutting off the lights, Cletus put the truck down into granny low and slowly crossed the shallow creek dividing the fields. The tiny lights there flickered and seemed to move in slow circles. The night air seemed to echo and gentle chanting like a soft humming was coming from the dark farmhouse. Cletus restarted his chariot and drove toward the old silo.

Oatis reached down and patted Cletus's shoulder; "I heard about stuff like this, man. I think it's some aliens. Saw it on TV last night; they making' circles and abducting' folks and mistreating' cattle all over the place. Man, you got them right here on Uncle Ben's place! What we gonna do, Cletus? We gotta think of our kin, why they could be next! This might be some invasion force, and it's up to us!"

Cletus listened to his friends' sage advice and slowed the big truck down to a crawl. A large grove of pines stood between them and the lights still circling slowly just beyond. He put the Dodge in park and shut off the engine.

Turning towards the guys he whispered, "You're right; we might be the only thing between them and our families. Don't know bout you but I ain't about to let no outta town alien beings screw up my Christmas! I vote we get our guns out, go down, and take us a look. If it gets bad, we can get the guys from the lodge! What ya say? You guys in?"

Nodding heads and thumbs up from all. Almost without a sound, except for Billy Bob's cussing after dropping his thirty aught six in the mud, they gathered up the supplies.

The snow was heavy and melting, mud mixing with the slush as they worked their selves closer to the circling lights. The humming sound turned out to be voices and they could now see exactly what the lights were coming from.

"Cletus, look at that! It's a Klan meeting' or something! " Billy Bob whispered.

There before them stood a group of a dozen or so people in white flowing gowns, dancing slowly around the burnt out hulk of Uncle Bens old round, used to be feed bin, a.k.a. hidden still. Well, that was before it burnt down anyway. The only remaining thing there was a tall half-baked oak tree and part of a concrete wall. They danced and chanted as they circled it. Each hooded figure carried a small candle and continued chanting as they moved.

LeRoy tapped Cletus on the shoulder again," I heard about this stuff. Why, back in the thirties my papaw told me they burned a cross in his front yard. We don't want them kind moving in here."

Cletus pulled his shotgun up and checked its shells. "No way, LeRoy! They ran them types outta here years back! Ain't gonna have them sneaking back in now. It's gonna be up to us to stop it right here. You boys up to it? They might be packing' iron."

Each one nodded in agreement and Oatis whispered. "Here, have a slug of Oh Be Joyful, boys. We gonna need us a tad of courage in a bottle for this one. We might not make it out alive, you know. Sides that it will warm us up a bit. This battle might just last all night!"

Oatis slid the glass flask out of his overalls rear pocket and unscrewed it. Each took a turn for a quick sip of the brown fire. Cletus handed the bottle back and took a deep breath. "Okay boys, this is it. Let's move slow and try to get as close as we can without getting spotted."

The chanting became louder and then they watched as a heavyset person reverently touched the half-dead tree and removed her hood. She was pretty well rounded with long black curly hair flowing all around her face, and a voice like nobody there had ever heard. "Vee haff gathered here, dear brothers and sisters to celebrate this glorious day! Dah! A day of new beginnings! It iss our time uff celebration. Yah, uff Solstice!"

Her words echoed and LeRoy nudged Oatis with his elbow whispering," What the hell is a Salsa celebration? This just ain't right."

"Shhh," Cletus whispered. "I think it's some Mexican thing, unless the KKK's gone and changed something the news ain't told us about. Lookie there, they're all singing again and what the hell! They're playing' a flute!"

The hefty woman circled the tree, dancing and whirling about it. Her hair had twigs of evergreen in it and soon all the people were swirling about her. Black Billy lowered his gun whispering, "I think they did change their membership. Why, that there guy holding that piece of tree and candle, why he's darker than me! We gotta run them off Cletus. This just ain't right. Why I ain't having' my family turning' into a bunch of hooded shroud wearing, cross burning' homeboy clan bangers! Now, where did I put that thirty foot cross we were going to toast in somebody's front yard tonight. I don't think so! "

LeRoy motioned towards the figures, "I think they're gypsies if ya ask me. My cousin Lucas, why they stole him. We ain't never seen him since either. They're worse than them aliens I hear!"

His words trailed off as the singing stopped. "I think they heard ya, LeRoy! Get ready boys, we been seen!"

All the robed figures slowed turned and faced the hunters still hiding in the brush. The heavyset woman moved towards them and smiled. She had a rich voice and a thick Russian sounding accent. "Pleasse. Come out dear friends! Do not be afraid. Von't you pleasse come join us in this, our celebration of life."

Hearing the Russian accent, Oatis slammed a double aught shell into the chamber of his Wing master twelve gauge. You know, there's no sound scary as that anywhere in the world. However, the robed ones paid no attention!

"LeRoy, Oatis, keep me covered an' I'll do the talking."

Cletus moved slowly towards the woman. "What'cha doing on my Uncle Ben's place Lady, or whatever ya are. You're not from around here, are ya?"

The woman laughed softly. "Vee haff recently purchased this land, dear friends. Vatt brinks you out on such a night like this? You're velcome all to join uss. It iss the vinter Solstice, a time for new beginnincks for the mother earf. Come!"

Cletus looked back at his friends whose rifles stayed steady on the robed woman.

"Why, we were hunting deer. Nobody told us Uncle Ben's place has been sold. Just what kinda meeting you got going on here, anyway?"

By now the other robed figures slowly moved towards the other hunters who had moved backwards until finally, they were back to back to each other. Oatis was grinding his teeth. "They not taking' me alive, Billy Bob. Who's with me? I ain't getting probed by these here things! They pulling the wool over our eyes I tell ya!"

A slender woman smiled at Oatis, then handed him a flower and her lit candle. Another woman took Billy Bob's hand and led him toward the fire. Another walked around with a tray covered in bright blue spotted mushrooms and other plants, offering them to the folks at the fire. Cletus watched as one by one his friends eased over to the fire to warm themselves. Only then did he recognize that they were all in mortal danger. "I don't know what you did to the guys! But this gotta stop right now."

The heavyset woman backed away and then moved aside to speak softly to Black Billy, smiling. Cletus stomped over to where LeRoy was eating more of the little blue mushrooms and chasing them with shots of liquor. "What are you doing? We gotta stop them!"

LeRoy handed his bottle to Cletus. "Relax buddy, they are just a bunch a salsa celebrators they tell me. I ain't eating any more of these mushrooms though. They have a nice twangy taste, but something about 'em ain't right. I can't feel my right leg, but I can hear my hair growing and I know it. Well, they gotta be city folks if ya ya ask me cause these ain't no morel's. And my pappy said ya never eat those other speckled ones cause, why your head might just end up somewhere else it ain't supposed to be.

My pappy's always right bout that stuff. He knows things. Why, they doing some 'initiations too, a little different from those at the lodge, but kinda the same. They call it Wiggan, and if ya ask me, they are a wiggin' out alright. But they look pretty harmless. Sides that, it's cold out here and I ain't seen hide nor hair of any deers. I seen what's under them there robes though and why, it's not a sight a sober man should have to see." He took a deep drink from the bottle and held it out to Cletus.

A skinny man with horn-rimmed glasses handed Cletus a piece of a tree and started singing again.

"LeRoy, I think you're right. Maybe they got ole Uncle Bens still working again or something. Anybody see any guns? Hey, where's little Black Billy, anyway? They got him I tell ya!"

Oatis got up from the tree stump he was using for a seat and pointed towards the barn. "Last time I seen Black Billy him and that fat lady was holding' hands and heading' off towards the barn. Says she's gonna show him something."

Cletus looked over at Billy Bob who was eating a hunk of meat off a skewer. "Ya ought not be eating that stuff Billy Bob; ya don't know who it is! It might be neighbor! It ain't right, boys. We're giving up too easy. They gonna take over the world while we sit here eating' and drinking' all night. We gotta get the sheriff."

LeRoy picked up his shotgun and patted his stomach.

"Was roast beef Cletus. I know me a cow when I eat one for sure. Don't think my stinking' neighbors would taste that good. It's getting late. I see the sun starting' to peak through the trees yonder. If I don't get home soon my ol' lady's gonna have the hide off me."

The gentle sound of a muffled engine interrupted the conversation. They watched as two or three sets of headlights moved closer. Cletus and LeRoy held the guns ready.

"Maybe it's the Sheriff." Whispered Leroy. Sleek and black new as a catalog picture, a Mercedes Benz stopped just beyond them, then a bright red Lexus parked next it. Robed figures exited the vehicles and walked towards them smiling.

"It has been wonderful, new and dear friends. But it is time for us to leave now. We'll be back with the next Solstice and maybe you can have your families join us. I have checked my satellite radio and the weather is fine for our trip back to the city. Email us sometime. It's always nice to know the neighbors! We just can't wait to move the commune here in the spring."

Cletus lowered the rifle and shook the skinny man's hand.

"Ah well, I suppose it's been fun to meet ya too. You're gonna come back? You're gonna start a what, a communist party?"

He looked over at LeRoy, who was swigging on the bottle and nodding, waving his arms like airplane wings, singing a vague song about sending some airmails. Without any other words, the robed ones got back in their cars and disappeared. Cletus saw the headlights of other cars as they turned onto the gravel road. Then he suddenly remembered that his friend was in danger.

"They got Billy! Come on you guys! We better git back and call the sheriff! They gonna start a communist party, I heard it myself."

Oatis stumbled towards them with Billy Bob in tow. The big Dodge sat half buried in the sludge. Cletus jumped in the front and fired up the big V8 and in a minute they were throwing mud six feet in the air working their way back across the fields.

He stopped just beyond his gravel drive and shut off the engine and lights.

"Okay guys, we gotta think up a real good lie. If I go telling Brenda Sue we was partying with a bunch of commie wiggan druid tree huggers, she's gonna know I been drinking something I shouldn't."

LeRoy opened the cooler and handed another beer to Cletus.

"She gonna know something's up anyway. We gotta call the sheriff about Black Billy and she's not gonna take that sitting down. Him and his maw have always been the best neighbors you and Brenda Sue ever had, and here we got him killed! There ain't no way we got a good enough line of crap to get us outta this one, Cletus."

Cletus tipped the can and swallowed hard. "I got it. First gimme another one of them Buds. Okay, here's what we do. When we get in the yard, Oatis, you flatten the tire. See we had a flat, then LeRoy, you get to hollering about little Black Billy being' lost in the woods. Billy Bob, you just go along, and we can get outta this; we got to stick together."

The big V8 fired up and slowly they moved down the gravel into the long steep drive. The porch light flicked off. He knew she would be waiting. The sun was shining brightly through the eastern morning sky now.

He shut the engine off and Oatis slipped out of the truck bed unnoticed, screwdriver in hand and slammed into the rear tire. Cletus heard the hissing and opening the truck door, his eyes opened wide with surprise. "I said the spare tire, ya moron! That's the only new tire I got. The spares in the back, you was sitting on it!"

Oatis frowned and grinned almost at the same time. The screwdriver quickly slid into a rear pocket. There in the doorway, in a gray white housecoat that should have been thrown away last year and pink bunny slippers stood the love of his life.

Then the awkward morning silence was broken by a roaring engine sounding like a V8 on them there steroids you hear about. Coming across the field with mud flying twenty feet up was the biggest blackest sweetest dream of a flying throne a good old redneck boy like him ever saw. A Hummer! Like the ads for the army. He just knew it was the government. It had to be! There was nowhere to run! There's Brenda Sue there in front of him and the men in black he always reads about at the grocery checkout. Those newspapers know everything about things like him and his friends had been doing, and now he would become just another missing person.

LeRoy ducked around the side of the Dodge and stood between Cletus and Brenda Sue. The black machine stopped just a few feet from them all. The windows were tinted black to hide the victims soon to be lost forever. The door slowly began to open and they saw a hand. A black man's hand.

"Why, hi ya guys! I got me a ride back here. Seems Miss Linda was going this way and ah, offered me a ride."

Cletus walked over to Black Billy, smiling there at the open door. Looking inside he saw the heavyset Russian woman covered in dry leaves and golden pieces of straw entangled in her long black disheveled hair.

LeRoy slapped Billy on the shoulder, smiling. "See if your friend can give us a ride home. Seems Cletus has a flat and no spare. Don't ask how."

Billy whispered something to the driver and then motioned towards his friends shivering in the front yard.

"She says sure. It's a neighborly thing to do. Cletus, we'll see ya tomorrow. Come on guys! This thing is even badder than Cletus's Dodge!"

Cletus stood there and watched as all his friends deserted him. Brenda Sue watched from the screen door.

"Cletus honey. Why don't ya come on in here, Darlin'?" You just tell me all about it. It's okay. After what I just saw, I think I can just about believe anything you say this morning.

Cletus stomped his muddy boots off at the door and looked over at the half-finished fireplace just there beside him.

"I think I'll get that finished for ya today, Honey."

The door closed quietly and soon the smell of fresh boiling coffee filled the morning air. Cletus pulled a chair up to the table and smiled at Brenda Sue.

"Well, you see, we started out going deer hunting you know and well…"

Chapter 3

Turkey Fishin'

Cletus hung up the phone and smiled, "Listen Brenda Sue, the hardware store still don't have the part in and well me and Otis saw us a bunch of Turkeys. Soon as it's in, you know I'll get it done. Look the snow was just a freak anyway, nice and dry out now. We still got us a week before Christmas." Brenda Sue shook her head and poured herself another coffee. "You go on, glad to get you out from underfoot. Bad enough with all six heathens home for the holidays. Now go on.

The siren stopped and the squad car pulled up behind Cletus's truck. Recognizing the plates, he moseyed over to the men hanging off the bridge. "Cletus why in damnation are you guys are hanging over this bridge with a lasso and a spotlight?"

Cletus climbed back on the railing and halfheartedly grinned. "Sorry Hoss, it's Otis's fault. We're just trying to catch my Johnboat before it crosses the Arkansas line. See, ah, well it kinda started out innocent enough.

"Are you sure this is where you saw all the turkey's Otis?"

Otis nodded and pointed again at the far side of the Current River. "Right there! More turkeys than I ever saw in my natural born put together. Watch right there. See them? Now lets get your boat down and cross on over. There's so many, we can pick them off with twenty-twos!"

Cletus and the boys pushed the boat in the river, threw in the guns and beer and shoved off.

"Otis! You're right! There's hundreds of them! We gonna go home with a record breaking beard tonight!"

Little Black Billy popped the tops on some brews and handed them out to his partners, "My ole lady just ain't gonna believe, we got us a limit on turkeys in an hour. Lets just kick back and have a few before we get started harvesting!"

The trolling motor moved the boat in a straight line towards the opposite shore. The birds seemed to mull about unaware of the danger awaiting them. Cletus took out his twenty-two and from the boat popped a huge male. "Why, I heard of shooting fish in a barrel but this is ridiculous, shooting turkeys from a boat! Lets get on in there and get us a few more!"

Otis jumped out of the boat and pulled it on shore, hurriedly tying it to a limb. They grabbed their guns and ran towards the flock of unsuspecting birds. Within minutes each stood with huge a Tom Turkey, each bird had a beard as long as a man's hand. "Hey Cletus. Let's put these in the boat and go inland a tad. Man, the big ones might be further in. What if they are just past the honeysuckles?"

Quicker than a hound dog on a rabbit, they threw the birds towards the front of the boat and disappeared into the brush.

Ten minutes hadn't past. You could hear the pop-pop sound of the twenty-twos as they made their mark.

Lumbering along the shoreline, grubbing for dead fish the young male brown bear smelled the blood. He stood on his hind legs and peered into the johnboat at the birds. Slowly placing one huge paw on the seat, then another he made his way into the front. His nose and paws recognized the treasure at the same moment. Feathers flew! From a distance, it was as if a brown mist encompassed the shoreline.

Otis headed back, bearing his latest kill and stopped just short of the beach. Slowly he backed up into the cover of the brush. Cletus and Black Billy almost slammed into him. Cletus pushed him; "What's the hold up? Come on! There's more birds out there, with my name on them!"

Otis shook his head and kept backing up. "You go on ahead. I ain't telling no bear he can't have our turkeys."

Cletus pushed past him and stood on the shore twenty foot from the boat. He dropped his birds and slowly backed up. "Okay Black Billy, got any ideas? Otis? We just can't stay on this side of the river all night while we wait for him to finish dinner ya know!"

Billy shook his head no then smiled; "I got it! Cletus, just pop him one with that there twenty-two! When he drops the turkey, we run for shore and steal the boat back! You do it Cletus! Just pop him in the ass one time! He'll run for sure!"

Cletus rubbed his chin and looked at Billy. "I'll pop him alright! Okay, when he runs, we all make for the boat! Hang onto the turkeys!"

.Cletus raised the rifle, squeezed the trigger, and the loud crack made the bear seem to jump three foot. It raised its head and screamed. All three men ran for cover in the brush. The bear ripped and tore at the cooler and seats. Brown feathers flew into the air like a whirlwind.

Otis leaned against the tree and he saw the sign. "Cletus, look there."

Cletus looked above his head at the sign half covered with new growth; "Magillicudy's Turkey Farm"

Otis watched the bear and Cletus's face and then smiled. "Man, I told ya they was here! I never saw no sign! We gotta get outta here, you guys!"

They could hear a tractor in the distance. The engine sound seemed closer. Cletus looked at the bear and then at his buddies. "Okay guys, we got the turkey farmer or the bear, which one you willing to face?"

They screamed, waved their arms and ran for the johnboat at the same time.

The bear still angry over the gunshot stood part way on shore and in the water. Seeing the men, it darted into the boat again. Its weight caused the johnboat to push further out into the water where the current caught it, and the boat quickly headed down river. Cletus stood there his jaw hanging open. "Swim for it boys! We can get the boat if we catch it at the bridge!"

Otis jumped into the freezing spring fed river and began to swim; he shivered a question to Cletus. "Where's the keys Cletus?"

Cletus swam harder watching the boat make the curve. "In the boat! Come on you guys! It won't be the first time I hot wired that ole Dodge!"

The three men lay on the shore gasping. The reds of the sun began to show in the southwestern sky. Cletus got on his knees and looked back at the guys and then at his beloved johnboat, slowly fading into the sunset!

Otis gulped water, coughed and hollered to Cletus; I got a spotlight and some rope! We can lasso that there boat before it hits the Arkansas state line, Cletus!"

"Well. Anyways Sheriff, that's the truth, and Cousin, have I got a deal for you! If you'll turn off them flashy lights on top of your squad car and ease it on back into town like you never even seen us tonight we scouts' honor promise that we won't never go turkey fishin' again. At least, not without you coming' along with us, that is! Thank you, Cuzzin. We are out of here!"

Chapter 4
Red Blooded American Food

"But Honey, I won the radio contest I gotta go!" Cletus gave her the saddest set of cow eyes he could work into. Brenda Sue smiled and handed him the plane tickets. "Honey I know ya won but ya'll ain't qualified to judge no Olympic thing. You go one, just call me from there okay?"

Cletus parked the ole Dodge at the airport and waited in line for them to get the security scans finished. The woman at the counter was nice until she found his Arkansas toothpick in his bag.

"Sir! You're not aloud to have weapons on board any flights! What is this exactly?"

She reached for the microphone to call security. Cletus gave her a partial toothless grin. "Listen lady. I am judging the cook off with the Olympics! I won it on the radio show." He handed her his papers and winning telegram.

"Sir, leave that with us. They'll have plenty of utensils for you there at the Olympics, no need to bring your own."

Cletus wasn't too worried he'd make more when he got home. The plane landed four hours later, the cook off was already in progress. The usher hurried him to the line where already food was lining up. Cletus stood there dumbfounded. He had never seen so much different varieties in his life.

The loud speaker called his name, introducing him to the crowd. "And will you welcome Cletus Somdummer from the Ozarks in Missouri!"

A small applaud followed. Cletus picked up a fork and looked at the first plate of food. He tried to read the card next to it.

"Filet Minion ala Grasses dume' slowly reaching into the mass of foreign sounding food he stopped at looked at the tall gentleman next to him. "Ya gonna tell me what this crap is, or is that what my job is?"

Tight lipped and frowning he tried to answer. "Your job is to read the card and tell whose food is best ya moron!"

Cletus squinted at him. "Back home boy, you'd be eating those words. Since this here's some contest I'll let it go, one time."

He tasted each piece and moved to the next platter. Cletus looked again and read the card

Frog legs, broiled rice with mushrooms

A tip of garlic

2 tsps. of Oregano

A dabble of minion Del grion

Cletus tried to figure that one out. "Tastes like frogs and rice to me boys, what the big deal?"

The next plate was covered in fresh sautéed Escargot. Cletus took his fork and poked at the small shells lying there motionless. The large broiled potato rolled off the plate and onto the table. Without thinking, he stabbed the rolling spud and slammed it onto the platter again. Its soft white center splattered the person next to him. Without a second thought, he picked up the potato on his own plate and slammed Cletus along the side of the head with it. The whole time hollering obscenities "You stupid backwoods hick! What do you think you're doing! This is being broadcast live!"

Cletus smiled again and wiped the mashed potatoes from his face. Still grinning he picked up the Escargot and looked inside the shell at the shriveled creature. He laid the fork on his plate and rolled up his sleeve. "Listen I promised Brenda Sue I'd be good on this trip. Well boy! I took about enough shit from the likes a you! Tell ya what! Why don't we just stuff these here fancy snails right up your big fat nose and see what happens!"

Cletus had a handful of them now moving towards him. The judge seeing the altercation moved behind the tables between them. Listen you two! Can't we be civilized about this?"

Cletus's smile grew even wider his eyes twinkled. "I can see that ya both are in cahoots! I tell ya what! Lets see what you both think when ya smelling snails for a week!"

A police officer slid across the table trying to get between Cletus and the two men.

"Cletus? Cuzzin! Is that you?"

Cletus quit smiling and looked into the officer's eyes. "Well damn my hide! Shucks son! What the hell ya doing here? Aunt Mame's been searching for ya high and low and here ya are right here at these here Limpic things! Why she gonna faint dead away!"

The police officer removed his glasses and smiled at Cletus. "Cuzzin, I tell ya what. You leave them there two city boys alone. I'll buy ya a bottle of the best lightening in town. How bout we just leave these guys to this here food and get going?"

Cletus popped a couple frog legs in his mouth and grabbed a bottle of Chardenieh from the table. "Hell, this ain't no food contest. They eating frogs, grass, and even slug snails! Lets go on over to the burger house. This ain't worth staying for."

The room was silent. A reporter from the Time's clicked open his cell phone, the musical sounds of the dial echoing through the room. "Desk, front page. Olympic judge gets sick from entries. Local burger house attested, by him as best in world. Okay you get that? Yeah. I'll get photos."

The other entries stood there looking at the reporter. He slipped his phone in his jacket and shook his head. "You folks have lost your marbles if you thought a red blooded American was going to eat that stuff. I'm going to the burger joint."

Brenda Sue flipped on the TV. There was Cletus eating at a roadside restaurant. Putting her hands on her hips, she bit her lip and squinted her eyes. "He better have a good lie for this one let me tell you!"

Chapter 4
Cuzzin Homer's Art

My assignment was simple enough, The Greater Saint Louisa Art Council and Center had made it clear, somewhere west of the city resided Homer Sumdummer. Homer's art began to show up all the way to New York and my job was to find out why we had never heard of him. Photographs of his art had circulated throughout the galleries they resembled some kind of metal sculpture; the gallery had decided to procure some for their own. The road from the city on the interstate seemed very uneventful until he took the exit. The map listed Mr. Sumdummer's small town only 100 miles west of here. So, I headed west.

The four lane turned to a two lane and the two lane turned to single. I found a small convenience store at the corner of Opossum and route A. Thinking that I had to be lost, I went in to ask for directions. When out of my turf I'm not proud, it's not my idea of fun to roam around waiting for the destination to appear. I might live in the city but I am not a moron. Or so I thought.

"Mam, I'm trying to find a Mr. Homer Sumdummer's place of residence. If you'd be so kind, have you any idea where it is or maybe how to get to Raccoon drive?"

She finished wiping out the thick mug and smiled at me. "Well, I be darned, bet ya'll bought that crap he been selling out east ain't ya?"

My stomach began to jitter when I realized she knew him. "Why I'm here from the galleries in St. Louisa. We believe that it would be to his benefit and ours if a professional critique were made of his work. We think we can help his career and further the advancement of the arts."

She grinned again and tried not to laugh but I could tell it was hard. "Why you just head over to the holler about 3 miles back yonder, she pointed at a gravel road across from her small store. Well, he been a might busy with all them there orders he got lately. But if'n he ain't home his cuzzin Cletus lives next door, he can help ya out some."

I laid a five-dollar bill on the counter for my bottle of water and nodded to her. "You keep the change mam, and thanks so much. You've done a service to the art community."

I walked back to the Mercedes and watched as a group of young children scurried away from my car. I backed out and pulled onto the gravel drive she had pointed out.

The road turned and turned again. Now it was a one-lane gravel road. I kept my speed to a crawl so to not cause a chip in the black shiny paint of my recently purchased piece of happiness. Then ahead of me, I saw the road seem to go straight up. I had to accelerate so that I would not have to have to down shift before reaching the top. As quickly, as it rose the same road fell straight down and then curved. My heart raced. I had never driven on such a piece of road before. I could not believe that my tax dollars went to roads like this.

Without any warning, the road made a sharp left. I hurriedly turned the wheel and slowly pressed on the brakes, I could hear the gravel dancing off my wonderful car. I tried to put the image of dents and chips out of my mind. I looked down at the speedometer and I was now traveling at an enormous racing speed of ten miles an hour. The sky behind me gathered a gentle orange glow. Night was fast approaching and here I was fourteen miles down raccoon road with not a house in sight.

Suddenly right in the middle of the road sat a huge logging truck, I had nowhere to go. I saw his flashing yellow lights and slammed on the brakes. I had no idea that a car would swerve and skid at a lousy ten miles and hour. I could hear the screeching of my brakes and my knuckles turned white. It seemed like hours but finally within a few feet of a huge oak log, the Mercedes stopped. I just could not seem to let go of the steering wheel. I tried to catch my breath. Then from the corner of my eye, I spotted a man.

He walked towards the car and me. I saw him spit a gob of some disgusting brown liquid from between his teeth. He bent down and looked into my window.

"Ya'll got a problem with this here vehicle? Ya need some help there boy?"

I started to roll up the window; the power window did not budge. I smiled and lied.

"Well, I must have taken a wrong turn sir. I was on an assignment to interview a Mr. Homer Sumdummer when somehow I took a wrong turn."

The man spit again, his thumbs lodged on the straps of his blue overalls. He leaned back on his heels and grinned. "Why sonny, ya ain't lost at all. Cuzzin Homer his place a bout half mile yonder. Just go on around my truck here. Ya will see his place directly."

I thanked him and started the car. Slowly I inched my vehicle past the load of logs blacking the road. I looked over to my left and seemed like I could see for miles. I knew it was an illusion. There are no mountain passes in Missouri. I heard the sound of gravel as it echoed down the cliff beside me. Finally, I made it past the truck. The sky grew darker and before long, even the oranges of the sunset disappeared. Then I saw it a faint light in the distance. My headlights flickered. Time was running out. Scenes from Deliverance danced in my brain.

Finally, the dim light grew brighter; the front porch of a raggedy cabin came into view. There was a huge Dodge pick up parked and an ole Chevy on blocks off to the side yard. Fourteen huge dogs raced towards me. I parked the Mercedes and watched the front door. I knew they had to have heard the commotion all these damn dogs made.

Suddenly the screen door flew open and a tiny woman stomped onto the porch. "All right! I got myself two eyes to see ya bunch of morons! Now ya'll git on away from that there car! Right this minute."

Like trained dogs, tails between their legs they ran for the back yard. She sauntered towards me and had a smile on her face. "So, you can get out now iffin' ya want to ya know. They ain't comin back."

Rolling down the window I grinned. "Sorry to bother you Mam. I am looking for a Mr. Sumdummer. Would you happen to know if he lives close by? I'm afraid I'm quite lost."

Her eyes twinkled and she smiled broadly.

"Why you're in the right place boy. Just come on in. Homer should be here anytime now. Had to mail off another one of his dumb art projects. Should be back any minute now. He was stopping over at Cletus's house. Less'n those two been tippin the shine."

I opened the car door and followed her toward the door. I saw a large black dog peek around the edge of the porch and started to turn for the car. She saw it too.

"If I got to tell ya again dog! Your gonna wish'n ya was back in town where I found ya. Now get your dog ass back in the back yard this minute."

I swear the dog yelped as if she hit it with a switch. I hurried behind her and quickly we were inside. She motioned at a bright orange and brown ancient looking sofa. "You just sit on down there now. Let me get ya a tall glass of lemonade. How's that sound?"

I nodded. Then there was a sound like roaring engines and cackling mufflers. I glanced out her front window and in pulled a bright red brand new pick up truck. A stout little man in blue overalls slammed the door and headed towards the door.

She sat a glass in front of me and went back toward the kitchen. "Let me get Homer a cold one dear. You just sit tight, he'll be right in."

I peered out at Homer. He stood next to my Mercedes and bent down touching their hubcaps. All I could think of is how damaged they must be by now.

Homer turned and moved up the stairs; all the dogs began barking and jumping on him. He laughed and horded his way through the tangle of canines.

The screen door slammed again and there he stood. Five foot four inches I would guess of pure humor. I tried to picture this man as the famous artist I had came to interview. It just didn't seem possible. She handed him a tall can of beer and he smiled at me.

"So you here to pick up that order for that fella over in Kansas City? Hey that's a mighty fine car ya got out there. Weren't too smart bringing it up to these parts though. Sorry bout those pock marks on it."

My heart raced when he said pockmarks. My beautiful car!

"Well, Mr. Sumdummer. I have been sent by the art community to take a look at some of your work and do a story on you. This can be the beginning of a whole new career for you!"

Homer picked up my glass of lemonade and sniffed it. "Dang it woman! Go get this man a cold one. He don't want no sissy drink!" She shook her head, picked up my glass and disappeared into the kitchen, returning with two more cans. Homer sat across from me and propped his feet up on a box of magazines. "So what exactly they gonna offer me? I don't need much more sales ya know. Why this whole mess been good so far. Ya'll like my new truck? I sold me two dozen of em to get that there truck. You do any better than that?"

I looked out at the shiny new machine and shook my head in disagreement.

"Why no Mr. Sumdummer. We're going to help you get famous! When were done you will be world renown. You can double the price of your art!"

Home finished the tall can, burped and popped another one. "Why son, I don't need to be world famous. Why tar nation. I can't keep up with the orders I got. What makes ya think I'd need any more than I got sonny?"

"Mr. Sumdummer, if I could see one of your pieces I'd love to tell you more."

Homer tipped back his head and finished the beer. "Sweetie, ya wanna bring us a couple more and throw that new one to me, would ya?"

I heard a giggle from the kitchen; Homer stood up and clapped his hands. "Hit me right here woman."

I saw it fly through the doorway. Like a flying saucer landing in the living room., a bright silver spinning, hubcap. I almost choked on my beer. Homer caught it shined it a bit on the front of his overalls. He then handed it to me.

My mind went blank. I drove all the way, facing logging trucks, packs of killer dogs. I had to ding up my Mercedes for a bunch of hubcaps.

I flipped the silvery hubcap over and almost fainted. The complete picture from the ceiling of the Sistine Chapel was there. Cut out in tiny minute details. Like a painter with a brush, this country bumpkin had accomplished a feat of art that I could not believe. I quickly tipped my can of beer and drank it all. "Homer, how did you do this? I've never seen anything like this in my life!"

Homer slapped me on the shoulder. "Why sonny, that's one of my mistakes there. I got lot better ones out in the shed. Kathy Lou. You get us a few more of them and we'll be in the shed."

I held on to the hubcap with all my might and followed him out the back door. This time the dogs ignored me. We reached a rickety old barn and he flipped a door opened and turned on the lights. There, floor to ceiling were hundreds of the hubcaps. Every make and model I could imagine hung there. Each with a different cut out of a master. On a small workbench lay a small pile of files and saws. Home picked up a shiny baby moon hubcap and tossed it like a Frisbee. It was the Mona Lisa. I held it to my chest. Homer started laughing.

"Them don't break easy boy. No worries! Tell ya what. You want them there two? I'll make ya a trade. What ya say?"

I nodded not even knowing what it is he wanted from me. At the moment, it did not matter. My mind saw dollar signs! I had discovered a master!

Homer stood near his wall of cutouts and started pointing.

"Well, that's a 57 Chevy there. Over here we got us a Cadillac, that ones from an ole Pontiac. I got me quite a collection. Don't ya think?"

I just kept nodding. He turned and headed back to the house. I stayed right on his heels. Kathy Lou stood at the door with two more beers. I eagerly took one, staying right on Homers heels. The whole house smelled great. I hadn't notice how hungry I was until the smell hit me. His wife set three places at the table as I sat across from Homer, hubcaps still in hand.

"Listen boy. Just lay them there things down, they'll be fine. Lets eat something and we can do some dickering after." Go ahead boy, just lay em on the chair there."

Like a two year old, I nodded and laid them down, trying very carefully not to ding my treasures.

Kathy Lou laid a huge roast on the table and a bowl of some kind of greens and more food than I could imagine two people could eat. Home grabbed her hand and she grabbed mine. Started I looked up.

"We say Grace in these here parts sonny. Ain't ya ever done that?"

I nodded and bowed my head. I have no idea what he said; my mind was still in high gear. Then I heard Amen.

"Okay sonny, how much meat ya want? A bit or a bunch?"

I stuttered and he just grinned.

"Here eat what ya can; dogs get some leftovers too then."

He heaped on a chunk of the meat, spooned green stuff, and baked potatoes. Kathy Lou laid a platter of fresh bread on the table and sat down. I watched them, nibbling at my food. The meat almost melted in my mouth. The green stuff covered in melted butter was as good as anything I had ever eaten at thirty bucks a plate. Finally, I couldn't touch another thing. I pushed my plate back and smiled.

"Why Mam, I have to tell you, that was a gourmet meal if I ever had one. I am curious, what was that wonderful roast?"

Homer cut off another hunk of the delicious roasted meat and grinned. "It's a Opossum boy. Ain't ya ever ate none before?"

I tried not to think of the last possum I saw, squashed on the highway. I picture Ham, Roast beef, any thing but a giant road rat.

Homer must have seen me turning green he pushed his chair back. "Come on boy. I got something fix yaw right up. Probably a bit rich for likes of ya, that all. Here have a slug of this."

He handed me a brown jug, he pulled a cork out of it and sat down. "Go ahead boy; it's made with fresh apples. Settle your stomach right down."

He was right. It was warm sweet with a touch of cinnamon. I tipped the jug again and swallowed four or five time. Homer slapped his knew.

"Easy sonny, it's gonna hit ya quick that way. Now why don't we get some haggling done? You spend the night tonight. We got some comforters and you can head out first light. Tell you what, you trade me four banged up hubcaps you got out yonder in the drive there and I'll throw in four more of my good ones. How's that sound?

By now I was feeling pretty good. The moon shone through the window reflecting off my car. What are four hubcaps worth compared to what I saw. It was getting very warm. I felt perspiration running down my face. Homer snickered.

"It's okay sonny. It'll pass soon. That stuff warm ya right up don't it. Ya gotta admit nothing ailing ya now. Is there?"

I grinned and started laughing.

"Why you can have those four old things Homer. That's a great trade if you ask me. I think I will take you up on spending the night though. I don' think I could find my way off this mountain of yours anyway. Why I love it here. What a great life!"

Homer must have known what was coming next. Here it is, sunshine blinding me. The smell of coffee was emanating from everywhere. I have died. I open my eyes and the minute the bright light hit them my head began to pound like someone is playing with a jackhammer. I squint and look around me. Two huge dogs lay sound asleep on my feet. There a cat on my pillow and Kathy Lou is standing there above me with a huge smile.

"Homer didn't want to wake you. You almost slept the day away. It is seven o'clock sleepy head. Here's a cup of coffee. I put a bit of the hair of the dog that bit ya in it. That'll stop the pounding."

I slowly sat up, the dog grumbled the cat stretched and I took a sip of the wonderful brew. Hot coffee, stout and sweet, a hint of apple. Soon the smell of bacon was everywhere, my stomach growled. I slowly stood up, adjusting my shirt. My headache slowly dissipating into the coffee aroma. She patted the table. There were four eggs and huge slice of ham and more coffee.

I can't remember eating like that since. She had my precious cargo nicely wrapped and a stack of four more waiting for me. I felt like a man who had just discovered a goldmine. I thanked her and headed to my car. Huge marks from the window down to the ground where the dogs had jumped on the car. There were hundreds of dings and chips all along the side of my precious car. Now there were four less hubcaps.

I opened the truck and laid the hubcaps inside, gently covering them. Kathy Lou brought a paper bag to the car. "Homer wanted me to send you some leftovers from supper last night. I also put a Mason jar of some stomach medicine it to. I'd keep it in the trunk if'n I was you. Don't need Johnny Law checking you while you're on your way home now do we."

I reached out and took her hand; she pulled me close and gave me a big hug.

"Homer said give ya a hug and tell ya, come back any-ole time ya want. He's a bit behind on orders so he won't have no more for ya for bout six months, just so ya know. You bring him some more trade goods and he'll get you some more goodies. "

She let go of me and I got in the car. The engine purred like always. I waved and backed out onto the gravel road. I tried to roll the window down but the electrics were frozen. I opened the door; "Tell Homer that was the best time I have ever had Kathy Lou. I'll get him lots more fancy hubcaps when I come back."

She waved. I slowly headed back to the city with my treasure. No one would ever believe me. I thought about how many hubcaps were parked in the Gallery lot and grinned. "Wouldn't Homer have a field day?"

The end

Made in the USA
Columbia, SC
02 May 2023